54-9992

The Seminoles:
Dwellers of the Everglades

BY WILLIAM C. EMERSON

Stories and Spirituals of the Negro Slave

The Seminoles: Dwellers of the Everglades

The Seminoles:
Dwellers of the Everglades

The Land, History and Culture
of the Florida Indians

by

WILLIAM C. EMERSON, M.D.

With 32 photographs

EXPOSITION PRESS · NEW YORK

To my two sons
WILLIAM HARRY EMERSON
and
HENRY RALPH EMERSON

Contents

St. Augustine, Florida

There liest thou, little city of the deep,
And always hearest the unceasing sound
By day and night, in summer and in frost,
The roar of waters on thy coral shore.

RALPH WALDO EMERSON

Introduction

Florida has ever been the land of change. The peninsula, built up of coral centuries ago, contains the oldest town in the continental United States. The history, the romance, and the culture of this portion of our country has intrigued poets, philosophers, naturalists, and archeologists since the days of the early Spanish explorers.

Much has been written about the beauty, the climate, the flowers, birds, animals, and inhabitants of this enchanting state. As the centuries have passed, this bit of coral thrust from the depths has taken on new meaning for mankind. The peninsula, once a bare coral reef, has blossomed and bloomed as no other portion of our country.

The original inhabitants have disappeared, remaining only as a legend. Their bones, covered by mounds of sand, are all that is left of this once-proud race. Other Indians, the Seminoles, driven by the white man from their homes in Georgia, now occupy the land once inhabited by the people who greeted the Spaniards with offerings of cocoa plums, venison, and the bud of the cabbage palm.

These Indians, the Seminoles, are the remains of countless thousands who, to gain their freedom, ran away from the hardships imposed on them by the white man in the early part of the eighteenth century. They fled to the Everglades and there stood and fought the white man. A proud race, the Seminoles, seeking only to be left alone in the vastness of the Everglades, have through a period of nearly two hundred and fifty years maintained their spirit, their culture, their language, and their tribal laws intact. Only a few hundred in number some fifty years ago, they have increased to 846 at the present time. They also have preserved their individuality as no other Indian tribe has. An extremely interesting people, they no longer live isolated on their hammocks in the interior of the Everglades, but more and more they are mingling with the white man.

In order to show how these people live at the present time, the country in which they live, the Everglades, and a short history of their predecessors, this account and these photographs are presented.

PART ONE

Florida Indians and Indian Lands

Tropical Everglades

BY LYNN RUSSEL

Ah, save these hammocks, plains and Everglades
    Where nature scatters beauty everywhere;
Preserve this land where grandeur never fades
    And open it for all mankind to share.

There is no finer Eden to be found,
    For here the tropic weaves her choicest spell;
Protect the birds that everywhere abound
    And here again let bright flamingos dwell.

Let laughter ring along the shell-strewn beach
    Where palms look down upon Cape Sable's coast;
Place loveliness within the nation's reach
    For grandeur is an ever welcome host.

Give pleasure to the ones who love the sight
    Of silvered lakes and tangled mangrove shores;
Who long to see the egret's graceful flight
    Or find rare plants within the jungle doors.

It were a crime to wantonly destroy
    The trees and flowers of this wonderland;
It were a sin if man, in cruel joy,
    Should kill for sport the few rare birds at hand.

Protect these lands and time will be a slave;
    There will be joy in every orchid's smile,
And God will laugh from every tree and wave,
    Rejoicing in a victory worth while.

CHAPTER I

The Everglades, Home of the Seminoles

The present name *Everglades* came into general use only after the acquisition of Florida by the United States from Spain in 1819. The Turner map of 1823 was the first to use the word *Everglades*. The word *glade*, of old English origin, comes from the Anglo-Saxon *glæd*, meaning "shining" or "bright as water." The English for many hundreds of years used the word to mean an open grassy place in the forest. In the early American colonies the word was used to mean stretches of grassy pasture. The Indians named the Everglades *Pa-hay-okee*, "the Grassy Waters."

The Everglades is a rock-bottom shallow basin about 170 miles long and 50 miles wide. Starting from Lake Okeechobee in south-central Florida, the grass flows like a vast body of water down to the southernmost tip of the United States mainland. Taller than a man in places, it stretches for 3,600 square miles of open wilderness broken only by clumps of live oaks, palmettos, and gumbo-limbo trees which form "hammocks," named by the Indians and meaning "floating vegetation." The true Everglades, according to the opinion of some writers, lie within a rock rim south of Lake Okeechobee. The large marshy territory south and east of Lake Kissimmee is considered part of the Everglades.

The Everglades rest on a foundation of limestone that dips toward the south. The basin is pitted with potholes and jagged ridges, and was at one time open sea. Wind and water carried in sand until the water was shallow enough for plant life to grow. By constant accretion through a period of many years, the basin has been filled to the level of the rock rim with deposits of sand and muck.

The phenomenon of the Everglades is due to the fact that the floor is porous limestone. In summer the floor is covered with a carpet of water, giving life to the grass; but in the dry season the water seeps down through the rock, and only grass that survives both flood and drought can live.

The black muck soil of the Everglades, the residue of centuries of rotting vegetation, is very fertile. Large areas have been cleared and planted to string beans, cabbage, sugar cane, tomatoes, and strawberries, which are sold locally and in northern markets.

After 1903, when Florida obtained title to the Everglades from the Federal Government, an attempt was made to reclaim portions of the huge swamp. In 1905 the Florida legislature authorized the Everglades drainage district and in 1906 drainage operations began. The first problem was to gain control over the waters of Lake Okeechobee, which inundated the territory to the south of the lake. The southern end of the lake was rimmed with dikes, and canals were dug radiating from the lake to both the Atlantic Ocean and the Gulf of Mexico. The main arteries are the Hillsborough West Palm Beach North New River and Miami canals, which are joined by many smaller channels and ditches to increase the flow of water and drain this region. The Cross-State Canal, navigable by ships of six feet draft, has been constructed by joining the St. Lucie Canal, which extends from Stuart to Lake Okeechobee, with a channel across the lake to Moore Haven. Here a channel with a lock leads to Lake Hipochee, the headwaters of the Caloosahatchee River, down which the water proceeds to the Gulf of Mexico.

Through this extensive drainage system vast areas of the Everglades around Moore Haven, Lockport, and Okeechobee have been converted into land suitable for growing beans, peas, sugar cane, lettuce, cabbage, tomatoes, and strawberries.

The margins of the Everglades, especially the northern margin, are fringed with pinelands, prairies, and hammocks. This open range country with its cowboys and herds of range cattle is reminiscent of the Old West.

The lower portion of the Everglades from about twenty miles north of the Tamiami Trail to Cape Sable on Florida Bay, except in small areas where canals have drained the Everglades, is unfit for cultivation. This vast area, called America's last frontier, is a last refuge for deer, otter, wild turkeys, panthers, bears, opossums, racoons, foxes, wildcats, spotted skunks, gray squirrels, marsh rabbits, cottontail rabbits, and water rats. Sea cows or manatees are found around the Ten Thousand Islands, and crocodiles are also found in this area.

In the canals, lakes, and swamps are alligators, bullfrogs, water snakes, water moccasins, terrapins, snapping turtles, and soft-shelled turtles. On the higher ground around the hammocks are rattlesnakes, cottonmouth moccasins, black snakes, indigo snakes, orange rat snakes, king snakes, and the deadly coral snakes.

There are many beautiful birds found in this area. Herons, egrets, coots, gallinules, rails, wood ibis, and white ibis are found in the canals and marshes. There are also hawks, buzzards, bald eagles, redbirds, mockingbirds, woodpeckers, red-winged blackbirds, doves, warblers, and quail found in the brush- and pineland. In the lakes and canals are found black bass, bream, catfish, garfish, mudfish, perch, and eels. And throughout this vast area may be found many beautiful flowers, including native orchids.

On the northern border of this vast uncultivated area lies the Tamiami Trail. Captain J. F. Jaudon, of Ochopee, surveyed the Tamiami Trail in 1916. Construction of the road proceeded slowly because of the labor shortage during World War I. The success of the project was still in doubt in 1924, when at about that time the State Road Department took over construction. On April 25, 1928, the road was smooth and surfaced and was thrown open to traffic after costing thirteen million dollars.

On the north side of the road is the Tamiami Canal. From this canal rock and muck were taken to build the elevated road. In the canal there are black bass, pike, perch, jack bream, shell cracker, catfish, turtles, snakes, and alligators. On the surface are dark-bodied white-banded teal and large brown mallards. Along the edges of the canal herons, egrets, white ibis, and sandhill cranes search for food. Kingfishers, crows, and buzzards poise on cypress limbs above the canal. If one looks closely in the grass along the canal, cottonmouth moccasins and rattlesnakes may be seen. (See Plate 2.)

The best places to see the wild life that abounds in the canal are from the many bridges. If one looks over the edge of one of these bridges, alligators, turtles, snakes, and an occasional otter may be seen.

On both sides of the Tamiami Trail, extending north from the canal and south from the highway, the Everglades

are overgrown with saw grass tough as bamboo with edges
razor-sharp. Out on the plains are hammocks overgrown with
scrub oak, willow, cypress, cabbage palmettos, and strangler
fig trees. Nothing stirs across these broad marshes. There is
nothing but utter desolation.

From Fort Myers to Miami fourteen Seminole Indian
villages are scattered along the Tamiami Trail, usually opposite gas stations. (See Plate 8.)

North of the Tamiami Trail the Big Cypress Swamp of
Collier County, embracing 4,000 square miles, is America's
largest swamp. It far exceeds the extent of the Dismal Swamp
in Virginia and the Okefenokee Swamp of Georgia and North
Florida. Here wide-buttressed trunks of cypress spread wide
at the base for greater support, and proceed upward for
quite a distance from the roots are knees, thought to be of
use in obtaining more air for the tree. The cypress tree grows
slowly, adding but one inch in thirty years to its radius.

The cypress is known as "the wood eternal," dating back
to the Ice Age. Specimens obtained from ancient rock forma-
tions are neither decayed nor petrified. The cypress tree is
the oldest living thing on earth, often attaining an age of
six thousand years. There is one cypress tree in Florida that
is thought to be three thousand years old.

Throughout the swamp is a profusion of Spanish moss,
air plants, and over a hundred varieties of ferns, some of
which have fronds ten to eighteen feet long (see Plate 32).

On the southwest corner of the Big Cypress Swamp is the
Collier Seminole State Park at Royal Palm Hammock in
Collier County. The park contains 6,423 acres, including the
Baron Collier Memorial Park. This jungle area on the fringe
of the Everglades extends from the Tamiami Trail to the
Ten Thousand Islands. The park was acquired by donation

in 1944 and remains undeveloped except for a small monument and caretaker's house.

Directly south of the Big Cypress Swamp and southeast of the Collier Seminole State Park is the Everglades National Park, which extends to Cape Sable. The suggestion to make this portion of the Everglades into a national park was made by Mr. Ernest F. Coe in 1928, and the National Park Service was in favor of the scheme.

In order to make a national park, the land had to be given outright by the State of Florida to the National Park Service. Governor Millard Caldwell in 1946 set up a National Park System, a state agency, with power to acquire land for the park. The commission found in the entire area about 189,000 acres suitable for agriculture; the rest was valueless for agriculture. The area was frozen against speculation in a Federal law called a "declaration of taking." A contract was drawn up between the Federal Government and the State of Florida and two million dollars deposited by the state to Federal credit by which the Federal Government could continue with the declaration of taking and complete the acquisition of the land. When on June 20, 1947, Governor Caldwell gave the check for two million dollars to the Secretary of the Interior, Julius A. Krug, the park was declared established.

The Everglades National Park now includes 1,280,000 acres. Additional acreage is expected to be added to the park, notably acreage north of the Tamiami Trail; that would impound the surface fresh water on which the wild life of the lower Everglades depend.

The Everglades National Park attracts many visitors. During 1952, more than 168,602 persons visited the park. This figure does not include those who came in by boat on any of the numerous canals or from Florida Bay. One may take advantage of the tours arranged by the Audubon Society of Miami, and self-guided tours have been inaugurated. Mimeographed folders are given to visitors as they enter the park by State Road 27 southwest of Homestead. Rangers are on duty from 9:30 A.M. to 6 P.M. daily at the entrance of the park. The folder shows all the routes by which the tourists may see the park. There is the Anhinga Trail, which Daniel B. Beard, park superintendent, says is best for seeing wild bird life. On other tours emphasis is placed on vegetation, history, or Indian life.

There are stations along each trail where motorists may stop and look around and, if they feel like it, climb small towers in order to obtain a better view of the area. One tour or trail leads thirty-three miles from the entrance to Coot Bay, where there is a snack bar. At Coot Bay there are chartered boats for those who wish to continue their exploration by water. Park naturalists conduct free walks at 11 A.M. and 3 P.M. daily from the Royal Palm Ranger Station near the Anhinga Trail.

Most of the Everglades is inaccessible by conventional means of transportation, and only on the highways and canals may tourists see the Everglades by means of automobiles and boats. The inaccessible portions of the Everglades may be reached by 'Glades buggies or by airboats.

A 'Glades buggy has three axles, two drive shafts, and ten tires. The middle and rear axles, each mounting four wheels, are independently driven through two transmissions connected in series. These buggies have sufficient traction for doing anything but climbing palm trees. When the going gets rough, cleats consisting of pieces of iron set laterally in chains are placed on the rear set of dual tires. These buggies must have special permission to enter the Everglades National Park.

The airboat is a shallow-draft craft driven by a sixty-five horsepower airplane engine with a pusher propeller, and it can travel through the Everglades at sixty miles an hour. (See Plate 5.) Airboats draw only two inches of water and do not need any water under certain conditions; they will run on grass that is wet from rain or dew. The regular cruising speed is from ten to twenty miles an hour. These boats are really the only craft that have the Everglades beaten, and they can travel much faster than the slower 'Glades buggies.

Froggers living near Palm Beach use such boats to hunt frogs at night. The bright lights on the airboat hypnotize frogs into waiting immobility until the frogger plucks them from the water with his spear. Airboats are also used for hunting alligators, when the season is open, and for taking tourists for rides on the Tamiami Canal along the north side of the Tamiami Trail.

The Everglades is a place of enchantment as well as a place of utter desolation, with its rippling sea of green saw grass that stretches away as far as the eye can see until it merges at last with the blue of the horizon. Those who enjoy the beauty of nature, who are thrilled at the sight of a deer, heron, or egret, would do well to spend days or even months exploring the vast areas of this part of Florida.

CHAPTER II

The Original Florida Indians, Predecessors of the Seminoles

When the Spaniards first arrived in Florida they found many Indians. However, since it is a well-known fact that they were prone to exaggerate everything they wrote, it is to be expected that they grossly exaggerated the number of Indians. They drew richly on their imaginations in describing tribal laws, culture, ceremonies, riches, and customs. Because they were dependent upon their Indian interpreters, we can not rely too much on the records of the Florida Indians left us by the early Spanish explorers.

To show how mixed up their descriptions are: they tell us that the Indians were cannibals and that the breasts of young maidens were considered delicacies reserved only for the chiefs. In other parts of their writings they state that in Peru and Florida cannibalism was unknown.

The first authentic description of the Florida Indians, left us by Ribault and Laudonnieri, describe mostly the tribes in northeastern Florida. They record three distinct confederacies of Indians in northern Florida: Satourtiona was the chief or king of one; Pataou was the chief of the second, and

Outina was the chief of the third. These Indians took the scalps of their enemies, and their arrows were tipped with bone. Their medicine men had great influence. The chiefs were carried in chairs born by four men with musicians playing on flutes, a custom that was typical of the Mexican, Central American, and Peruvian Indians.

We do know, from those records that appear authentic, that the Florida Indians appear to have been more closely affiliated with the South American and Mexican races than with the North American Indians. The custom of flaying their enemies alive and drying their skins as trophies was also a custom of the Mexicans. Their habit of drinking casiri, a beverage made from sweet potatoes, is part of a ceremony still used by the tribes of northern South America. The manner in which the Florida Indians combed their hair and tied it in a knot on top of their heads is more like the South American Indians than the North American Indians, and their tatooing and their feather crowns were similar to those of the south. There is a distinct possibility that the Florida Indians came from Mexico or South America.

This belief is in a manner confirmed by A. Hyatt Verill, in his book *Romantic and Historic Florida,* where he states that he has disinterred mummies from ancient graves in Peru arrayed in costumes similar to the Florida Seminole Indians'. There were the same full capes, long skirts, and mounds of beads similar to those worn by the Seminole women. There was also the same pattern in the woven cloth of the dresses, and the same colors were used. On the mummified bodies of the men were the same loose tunics, the same kiltlike skirts, and the same turban-like headdresses with the same kind of plumes, while resting on each sunken chest were three copper, silver, or golden plates of crescent form similar to those shown on the breast of the Seminole warrior Osceola.

If the Florida Indians were descended from the Incan tribes, the style and pattern of the costumes worn by their Peruvian ancestors two or three thousand years ago had been handed down from generation to generation; the costume was adopted by the Florida Seminole Indians when they mingled with the earlier Indians some two hundred and fifty years ago.

At the time of the early Spanish explorers the Florida Indians inhabited the entire state. In the southern portion of Florida, the extremity of the peninsula was divided between the Tegesta on the Atlantic and the Caloosa on the Gulf Coast, the latter territory extending south from Tampa Bay. In the northwest were the Apalachee Indians of Muskhogean stock who dwelt around the Pecillae River. South of St. Andrews Sound and the Cumberland River were the Gualean Indians. Up the coast toward Santa Elena, the northernmost part of Florida until 1558, were the Cussabo Indians, whose territory extended to St. Catherine's Islands in northern Georgia and on up into the Carolinas.

The fact remains that we know little or nothing of the Indians living in Florida three or four hundred years ago. These tribes, and no doubt others that we know nothing about, were completely wiped out. That is not hard to understand when we remember that for over two hundred years the Indians were killed like wild beasts and enslaved by the Spaniards. Hundreds were kidnaped and shipped to plantations and mines in the West Indies. It is a wonder that they survived at all and, unlike the Lucayans and Bahamas, were not completely destroyed and annihilated.

These Indians soon learned that the white man was not their friend, and they fought back savagely. Some of them (the number is not known) resisted complete annihilation by the Spaniards, British, French, and Americans. It is a legend among the Florida Seminole Indians that today there are a few of these Indians in the depths of the Everglades.

The truth is that we actually know less about the first Indian inhabitants of Florida than about any of the Indians who inhabited other portions of our country. Who they were and where they came from are questions that cannot be answered with accuracy.

All that we know about the culture and habits of the Florida Indians that is of any value has been learned from remains found in many mounds or burial grounds throughout Florida. From these findings we may conclude that the original inhabitants of Florida were wholly distinct from the Indians of more recent years. Archeologists have found that the tribes of the Creeks, Alabamas, Yamassee, and other tribes of the Algonquins are more recent arrivals, and that long before they came people with a distinct culture inhabited Florida. (See Plate 6.)

In the mounds or burial grounds were found ornamented clay vessels similar to those described by Alvar Núñez Cabeza de Vaca, who in 1528 stated that though the Indians of west Florida were very poor they had in front of their houses many clay pitchers of water. Some of them were very elaborate, with as many as five compartments built up into the form of a human or animal body and so fashioned that the head protruded and served as a handle. Most of these vessels were ornamented on the outside with a geometric design or drawing resembling a bird or animal. In many cases the lines were filled with some white substance in order to bring out the design more clearly.

Receptacles found in these mounds indicate a definite change in religious ideas over a period of time. One early custom was to break a hole in the bottom of the vase that was buried with the dead to kill the vessel so that its soul might escape and join the deceased. Vases thus destroyed were found in many burials. Sometimes the vases were placed over the skulls and sometimes they were buried in caches. Later it became the thrifty custom to construct, for burial purposes, an artistic reproduction of the vases with ready-made holes as part of the design. Among these were the best portrait vases found.

Archeologists found, besides vases, pottery. Pottery, for a long time, was the only way these Florida Indians could express their artistic ability. The first pottery was sand-tempered ware; then potters began to decorate their pottery. The Caloosas covered the rim with an over-all pattern of various feathered lines. The Tegesta Indians, living near the Miami River, used a crosshatching on their pottery, and the east-coast Indians used a paste to make a series of pottery called "Biscayne Ware." The Belle Glade Ware was developed by the Miami Lake Indians, while Indians living between what is now Fort Myers and Estero made pottery colored with red ocher on which they carved a paddle.

Skeletons of the Florida Indians around whose bodies the vases and pottery had been placed were found. Some of the bodies had their heads toward the center of the mound; others were flexed lying on one side with the folded legs at right angles to the vertebrae, and others were extended and lay either on one side or face upward.

The fact that bones were missing from some skeletons has led to the belief that these Indians removed the flesh from the bodies before burial, leaving only the ligaments to hold the bones together. This was done either by exposure to the weather or by cooking—a custom that has led some people to believe that the Florida Indians were cannibals. There is nothing, however, to prove that.

All these skeletons showed a very heavy bone structure, caused by the fact that they lived predominantly on a diet of sea food.

CHAPTER III

The Story of the Seminoles and the Seminole Wars

The Seminoles are not the original inhabitants of Florida but, rather, a mixed people consisting of remnants of the aborigines who survived the campaigns of Moore in the early 1700's or managed to escape enslavement, lower Creeks who migrated into Spanish territory, and Negro slaves.

In 1750 a large group of Creeks under Secoffee migrated south, settling in Alachua. Here they declared themselves separated from the Creeks and joined the Mikasukis. These Indians lived away from towns in forests, where they raised horses and cattle and cultivated orchards of peach, persimmon, and wild orange.

At the time of the Revolution the Florida Indians were known as *seminoles* meaning "separatists" or "runaways," and during the war were allies of the British. When the United States negotiated a treaty with the Creeks in 1790, an effort was made to force them to return their fugitive slaves; but the Seminoles denied any obligation to comply with the terms to which they were not a party, and the Creeks did not dare attempt violence on a people who did not recognize their authority. At this time the Seminoles did not even recognize the authority of Spain, but soon after the Revolution they made peace with Spain. The failure of the Spanish to meet American demands for control of the Seminoles was one of the talking points for the acquisition of Florida.

During the War of 1812 British influence again entered the councils of the Seminoles, who at that time were scattered through northern Florida. It was not surprising that when the Seminoles passed under the Stars and Stripes there was a heritage of grievances and old sores that made friction inevitable. During Jackson's campaign he urged the Seminoles to leave Florida and return north to their Creek kinsmen. When they refused, the part of Florida south of Charlotte Harbor, known as the Everglades, was agreed upon as the place for the Indians to live. The Seminoles were finally convinced that this was the place they should go, and the Treaty of Moultrie Creek was signed on September 18, 1823. Congress appropriated $65,700 for moving the Seminoles south and agreed to give the Seminoles $5,000 each year for twenty years. Unfortunately, the government agents got most of this money.

The land in the Everglades was not suitable for cultivation. There were not at that time any canals for drainage and the water of Lake Okeechobee inundated many hundreds of acres in that part of the Everglades. The reservation was twice extended, but even so, it was never large enough for the Seminoles. It is not surprising that Seminoles, hungry, homeless, and destitute, wandered north, stealing cattle, corn, and burning and looting the homes of the white settlers. For a time, they left their reservation in the Everglades.

While the Seminoles were wandering aimlessly through central and northern Florida looking for better homes and more food, the United States opened negotiations with the Creeks for removal west. When it became apparent that the United States could not confine the Seminoles in the reservation in the Everglades south of Charlotte Harbor, they were grouped with the Creeks in the plan for their migration westward. At a meeting between government agents and Seminole chiefs in October, 1828, at McKinzie's Pond the Indians agreed to send a delegation to investigate the western lands. They were told that they would not under any circumstances be forced to leave their lands or homes in Florida.

Four years drifted by and nothing happened on either side. Finally, on May 9, 1832, a treaty was signed by which the Seminoles relinquished their lands and agreed to migrate to the reservation assigned the Creeks west of the Mississippi River. One third were to go in 1833, one third in 1834, and the remaining in 1835. Seven chiefs went west to examine the country, and after their return a treaty was signed at Fort Gibson, Arkansas, approving the migration.

At about this time some white raiders kidnaped the beloved wife of a young Seminole named Osceola. Osceola went to Fort King and demanded justice from General Thompson. They would not listen to him; instead, he was arrested and thrown into prison. Released after twenty months in prison, Osceola was extremely bitter and bent all of his energies on reprisals and revenge.

Some of the leaders among the Seminoles favored moving west, among them Charlie Emalthla, chief of the Mikasukis. Having disposed of his cattle, Chief Charlie Emalthla was getting ready to leave with his family and tribe when Osceola appeared and killed him.

Other leaders among the Seminoles were not in favor of migrating to the reservation west of the Mississippi River. Among these leaders was Chief Micanopy, who accompanied

Osceola when he met General Thompson to sign still another treaty. General Thompson threatened the two Seminoles, telling them that if they did not sign at once the government would remove all aid and protection from the Indians at once and would regard them as outlaws to be shot on sight. At this point Osceola leaped up, pulled out his hunting knife, and, driving the knife through the treaty spread out on the desk, declared, "This is the only treaty we will ever make with the white men." Thus began the Seminole War.

The Indians took to the warpath everywhere, and on December 28, 1835, Osceola went to Fort King and killed General Thompson and his secretary, thus avenging the bad treatment received earlier when he went to see General Thompson after his wife had been kidnaped.

On the same day, the Dade massacre took place. With one hundred and ten United States regulars Major Dade had set out from Fort Brook (now Tampa) for Fort King (now Ocala), where he intended to join General Church and kill all the Seminoles in that area. As soon as the soldiers had crossed the Withlacooche River, guns roared from the surrounding jungle and men fell everywhere. Chief Micanopy killed Major Dade. The Seminoles did not take any scalps or search the bodies of the 108 men either killed or wounded, only taking guns and ammunition, but as soon as the Seminoles left some fugitive slaves appeared and killed the wounded soldiers.

The war continued with minor skirmishes. The Seminoles had about 1,000 men under arms, while the United States had about 18,000. On December 25, 1837, Colonel Zachary Taylor with 2,000 troops attacked the Seminoles encamped at the northern end of Lake Okeechobee. The battle began

Plate 1

The Everglades, a place of utter desolation, showing a plain of saw grass and a hammock in the distance.

Plate 2

The canal along the Tamiami Trail. In the canal there are bass, bream, catfish, turtles, snakes, and alligators; and herons, cranes, and ducks feed along the banks.

Plate 3

The Caloosahatchee River.

Plate 4

The Estero River.

Plate 5

An airboat like those used to hunt alligators and frogs.

Plate 6

An archeologist using a whisk broom to uncover a skeleton at the excavation of an Indian mound north of Vero Beach.

Plate 7

Seminole range riders in charge of one of the Indian herds of cattle.

Plate 8

A Seminole village on the Tamiami Trail near Miami.

Plate 9

Johnny Billie in his store at a Seminole village near the town of Everglades.

Plate 10

A Seminole woman making a dress. Like nearly every other Seminole woman, she has a hand-powered sewing machine.

Plate 11

A Seminole spearing a fish from a dugout canoe made from a cypress log. Note his bright-colored homemade shirt.

Plate 12

Two Seminole *chickees.*

Plate 13

A *chickee* showing sleeping arrangements. Unlike most Seminoles, this family sleeps on mattresses instead of only a bed roll.

Plate 14

A village of several *chickees* on the Brighton Indian Reservation.

Plate 15

The school on the Brighton Reservation.

Plate 16

Seminole children at the school on the Brighton Reservation. Note their bright-colored dress similar to that worn by their parents.

in the morning and lasted some eight hours, after which the Indians withdrew.

During several battles that followed, the Seminoles lost many men. The Indians were weary of war, and several of their chiefs expressed willingness and desire to sign a peace treaty. The United States, thinking the war over, removed most of the soldiers from Florida. Osceola, Chief Micanopy, and several other chiefs rallied about 700 Seminole warriors and fled into the Everglades. They did not attempt to renew hostilities; they were tired of war and simply wanted to be left alone.

On October 22, 1837, Osceola appeared under a flag of truce for a conference with General Hernandez at Three Pines, about seven miles from St. Augustine. When Osceola reached the appointed place he was seized, manacled, and taken as a prisoner to St. Augustine. This treachery aroused the people living in that part of Florida. Because there was considerable resentment against the United States Government, Osceola was transferred to Fort Moultrie in South Carolina, where he and two hundred other Seminole captives were imprisoned in cells and dungeons. Within a year Osceola died.

But this did not end the Seminole War. Coacooche (the Wild Cat), son of Chief Philip, and another chief, Talmus Hadjo, while visiting some sick relatives near St. Augustine were seized and placed in cells at Fort Marion. They starved themselves until they could squeeze their emaciated bodies between the bars of their cells, and they escaped. They lived on roots and berries and, though hunted by the white men, eluded their pursuers and joined their friends and relatives on the Tomoka River.

Deadly hatred was aroused in the breast of Coacooche, bitter at the treatment he had received, and again the Seminoles were on the warpath. This time the Seminoles were more aggressive. They held up a stage between St. Augustine and Picalata and killed all the occupants. A little later they held up a United States army wagon, killing all the occupants and departing with the loot. They carried their warfare to the gates of St. Augustine; for four years kept St. Augustine in a virtual state of siege and all of northern Florida in constant terror. Not until Coacooche was captured in 1842 did the people of Florida breathe easy again.

The Seminole War came to an end in 1842 when fifty Indians with twenty canoes were captured at Fort Lauderdale —the only victory of the United States in seven years of warfare. The Seminoles never admitted defeat. They had fought to retain their ancestral lands and to live unmolested in their own way in the Everglades. Some had been removed to western reservations, some had died in prison, and others had fallen in battle. However, the majority of the Seminoles still remained in possession of their homes in the Everglades where they still dwell. One tribe is still technically at war with the United States, because they have never signed a peace treaty.

In 1842 at the close of the war there were about 300 Indians living in the Everglades. Their reservation extended from the mouth of the Pecae Creek to the fork of its southern branch, from there to the head of Lake Istokpoga, down the Kissimmee River to Lake Okeechobee, through the Everglades to Shark River, and from there to the starting point.

In January, 1843, the two remaining chiefs, Sam Jones (Areika) and Billy Bowlegs (Holatter-Micco), announced that they had accepted the settlement made in 1842.

The Office of Indian Affairs in its report of January 20, 1844, summarized the Seminole removal. There were 3,824 Seminoles and Negroes who had been located in Arkansas and Oklahoma, but many Indians had died during the migration westward. Those Seminoles living in Oklahoma formed one of the five "civilized" tribes.

Following the close of the Seminole War there were sporadic uprisings and fighting between the Seminoles and troops sent by the United States to keep peace in the Everglades. Lieutenant Hartsuff, a civil engineer, ruined Billy Bowlegs' garden while making a survey of Florida. This provoked an Indian attack. The Government offered a reward of $100 to $500 for any Indian delivered alive at Fort Brook (now Tampa). Finally after three years of dodging his captors and intermittent warfare Billy Bowlegs and 150 of his followers went west.

Following Billy Bowlegs' migration peace again descended on the Everglades and has remained up to the present time. Today, the Seminoles, their ill treatment forgotten, live passively aloof, tenaciously adhering to their tribal ceremonies. They are bravely, doggedly fighting for existence, battling against the inroads of civilization, white men's diseases, and white men's rum.

CHAPTER IV

Osceola

A history of the Florida Seminole Indians and their wars with the United States would not be complete without a description of Osceola, the greatest of all the Seminoles.

Osceola, the guiding spirit of the Seminoles, was one of the bravest warriors who ever wore a plume or carried a quiver. He was born about 1800 on the Tallapoosa River in the Creek nation in what is now Georgia. His parentage is unknown. Legend has it that he was the son of William Powell, an English trader, and a comely squaw. According to another legend his mother was a white woman and his father a Creek. It is more likely, however, that he was of full Indian blood, for his features and conduct were characteristic.

As a young brave, Osceola fought against Andrew Jackson in the Creek War of 1812, and again in the Seminole War of 1818. Following the defeat of the Creeks in the battle of Horseshoe Bend, Osceola fled to Florida and joined the Seminoles. He lived near Fort King in Marion County.

Though not born of high rank and never chosen chief, Osceola had a commanding personality and by sheer force of strength and character became the acknowledged leader of his people through the Seminole Wars. His dauntless daring and savage cunning placed him in a position of authority. He hid the Indian women and children in the swamps and conducted guerrilla warfare with devastating effect, leading his warriors in surprise attacks and winning many victories. The unsigned treaty of 1834 still bears the scar where Osceola stuck his knife into it. Osceola, the elusive warrior, avoided every trap. His attacking braves fought in groups, and when surrounded, each followed in the track of the other until they reached trees, where they vanished.

Finally, after many years of fighting, Osceola was prevailed upon to talk things over with General Hernandez at St. Augustine, where he appeared on October 22, 1837, under a flag of truce, only to be seized and imprisoned in Fort Marion at St. Augustine. Public opinion was so aroused that he won the nation's sympathy, and because of sentiment in his favor, he was removed to Fort Moultrie in South Carolina for safekeeping.

Depressed, he refused food. Though joined by his two wives, he could not be comforted, and he died a year later on January 30, 1838. He was only thirty-eight, tall, strong and handsome, a perfect specimen of manhood. He had large, black, penetrating eyes and carried himself with regal dignity. Proud and courageous, he was of keen mind and strong convictions. He fought and died for what he believed was right. A man of mercy, he often warned his braves to spare women and children. "It is not to them that we make war," he said. "It is upon the men." Though severely wounded several times, he died of a broken heart.

Near the gate of Fort Moultrie a monument stands by the tomb of Osceola. Eighteen towns and cities and three counties bear his name, which in Creek means "rising sun."

Lakes, streets, and a mountain perpetuate his memory. His portrait hangs in the national Capitol, and as long as men are stirred by acts of heroism Osceola will be remembered as one of the great warriors of all time.

PART TWO

The Seminoles Today

Seminole Sleep Song

BY CARRIE BLAINE YEISER

Swing, Jonny-Willie, in your pretty red hammock,
  Frog in swamp make glad night song;
Alligator bay down in Big Cypress,
  Hammock hide Jonny when bear trot along.

Dark come quick when sun go down,
  Wind make music in tall pine tree;
Hammock swing out and hammock swing in,
  But sleep catch Jonny, he no can see.

Screech owl laugh and wildcat snarl,
  Bat swoop low, but Jonny no afraid,
Big chief tell: "No harm can come
  To Seminole baby in deep Everglade."

Swing, Jonny-Willie, in your pretty red hammock,
  Mockingbird call come low and sweet;
Stars make crown for your moss pillow,
  Moonbeam gild your little brown feet.

CHAPTER V

The People

The Seminoles in Florida today are divided into two tribes: the Muskogee, who live on the Brighton Indian Reservation north and east of Lake Okeechobee, and the Mikasuki, who occupy the Big Cypress Reservation south of Lake Okeechobee near the junction of the Everglades and the Big Cypress Swamp. Customs and habits vary, but to the casual observer there is little except dialect to distinguish the two tribes. The Muskogee Indians signed a peace treaty with the United States, while the Mikasuki Indians are still technically at war with the United States, having never signed a treaty.

All Seminoles have Indian names, but because few white men can pronounce them, each Indian has an English name —at least all men do. In most cases the name has nothing to do with relationship. The wives of most Seminoles have their husbands' names. Quite a few men bear the names of tribal heroes, such as Osceola and Billy Bowlegs, though they are not related in any way to these famous Seminoles.

One characteristic makes the Seminoles entirely different from the white man: no Seminole has what we call "the will to power." Individually, they do not wish to dominate. There is not such a thing as competition or rivalry in their society; ambition for one to win over another and the need to dominate are absent from their whole culture. All co-operate in whatever is to be done. When a *chickee* is to be built, no one is the boss.

This same characteristic applies to the method in which the children are brought up. Parents do not dominate their children. They never slap, correct, or inflict punishment on a child. Competition does not even play a part in the games of the children.

Certain misdeeds are punished, but this punishment is not imposed by the individual but by the tribal council; thus, no member of the tribe is stronger than another. The idea of getting the best of another fellow or of winning over another does not exist in Seminole society.

Seminoles do not display anxiety. In Seminole culture avoiding conflict plays an important role. Undesirable traits of character in someone are not dealt with by force. The pugnacious man is not acceptable to his fellow tribesmen; he is distrusted and feared.

Seminole belief in cause and effect is exemplified in their penal code. When a tribal law is broken, each person is assured of justice by the tribal council. That the welfare of the community is more important than the welfare of the individual leads to a stability of their culture and character. This may be derived from their inherent belief of the inevitable. If a Seminole does wrong, he receives his punishment without complaint. In no known instance has a Seminole tried to avoid or escape the sentence imposed upon him by the tribal council. The stoicism that every Seminole has to a marked degree may be derived from the utter desolation of the Everglades; each must accept conditions as they are without protest.

When a white man enters an Indian village, Seminoles are distinctly reticent in conversing, especially in answering questions. This reticence does not arise from any hostility, but rather from the inability on the part of many Seminoles to understand English. Indian women are forbidden by tribal law to talk to white men. But no case of a white visitor being insulted by a Seminole in his village or camp has ever been recorded.

The Seminoles are a moral people—much more so than the white man. There has been some slight lowering of the moral standard through contact with the white man, but even the missionaries on the Brighton and Big Cypress reservations find little to complain about.

The greatest vice among the Seminoles is drinking. They are born, grow up, and live in a monotonous country. Since there is not any place for them to go except to near-by towns, it is not any wonder that they break their dreary routine by drinking liquor. At times they consume large quantities of liquor and become quite drunk. However, drunkenness does not occur very often (during the time I spent with the Seminoles I saw only two drunken Indians).

Very few Seminoles smoke. Women do not smoke at all; men smoke cigarettes, pipes, and cigars occasionally.

There is not a tribe of healthier Indians in the United States than the Florida Seminoles. There are few cases of tuberculosis and very few cases of venereal diseases—one known case of tuberculosis during the past thirty years. In 1926 there were four cases of syphilis, one case of gonorrhea, and one case of typhoid fever. There are many cases of malaria, even though most Seminoles sleep under mosquito netting. The many cases of hookworm are caused by the fact that many Seminoles go barefooted and the sanitary conditions around their villages are not what they should be. The many cases of anemia are due to malaria and hookworm. But there have never been reported any cases of goiter or trachoma, so frequently found among other western Indians.

That there has never been a proved case of cancer among the Seminoles may be due to the low calcium content of their diet. It is a well known fact that there are very few recorded cases of cancer among the Eskimos and the people living in Africa, who also live on a diet with a low calcium content. The extremely good health of the Seminoles, like their longevity, may be attributed to their outdoor life, their easygoing dispositions, and their lack of worry and belief in the inevitable.

In contrast to their excellent health the Seminoles have very bad teeth, caused, in part, by a diet that consists principally of a gruel made of grits, ground corn, and stew with a noticeable lack of milk, fresh vegetables, and fresh fruit.

The Seminoles keep their bodies clean. They bathe often, and their clothing is washed and aired in the sun at proper intervals.

Childbirth is not the ordeal of prolonged agony it often is for the white woman. When the day approaches the Seminole woman builds a small palmetto shelter on a spot of dry land about two or three hundred yards from the village and drives a stake into the ground to grasp with her hands. If there is not another woman around to assist her, she has her child alone. At the present time very few Seminole women engage the services of a physician for childbirth, and no Seminole baby has been known to have been born in a hospital.

At the present time, if a Seminole becomes sick he may consult a doctor in a near-by town or city, for which consultation the Federal Government pays the doctor. If Seminoles require hospitalization, they go to hospitals in Fort Myers, in the town of Okeechobee, or in Miami; the Federal Government pays all the hospital expenses as well as doctors' fees. Today very few of the Seminoles consult the medicine men at times of illness or sickness, for most Seminoles prefer the services of the white doctors.

A public-health nurse at the Dania Indian Reservation assists the doctors in bringing patients to public hospitals and in carrying out a general health program including dental care in the villages and reservations.

CHAPTER VI

How and Where the Seminoles Live

There are three Seminole Indian Reservations in Florida.

The Brighton Reservation, located in Glades County, consists of 35,779 acres of grazing land with at least one fourth of the area covered with cabbage-palm hammocks. The sub-agency headquarters is located about seven miles south of the Brighton Post Office, some twenty-three miles southwest of Okeechobee City. About one hundred and fifty Seminoles live on the Brighton Reservation, but during certain seasons of the year they are gone for short periods. More than three thousand head of Indian-owned cattle are grazed on the reservation.

The Big Cypress Reservation, containing 42,613 acres, is located in the southeastern corner of Hendry County thirty-five miles from Immokalee. One hundred Seminoles live on the reservation, and many others come and go as they wish. Thirteen hundred head of Indian-owned cattle graze on the reservation.

The Dania Reservation, in Broward County about twenty miles north of Miami, contains 475 acres and fifteen Seminole families. There is a public-health nurse at the Dania Reservation.

Other Seminole Indians live in villages on the Tamiami Trail (see Plate 8), in an Indian village in Miami, in villages scattered throughout the Everglades, and in one small Indian village at Silver Springs, outside the Everglades.

The Seminoles do not receive any money from the Government and therefore must earn their own livelihood. When they first migrated to Florida, they lived in the same manner as other Indians living in the North American continent— by fishing, hunting, and raising corn and potatoes on cleared plots of ground near their villages. At the present time, however, because of the inroads of the white man, there is a scarcity of the game and fish.

The Indians on the Brighton and the Big Cypress Indian reservations were furnished herds of improved beef cattle in 1936 by the Government. These herds have increased under the management of trained extension workers who supervise and instruct the Seminoles in herd management. A Seminole may borrow ten head of cattle, but must put them back over a period of about eleven years. The affairs of the herd are managed by three Seminoles elected by the tribe.

There are 3,000 head of fine Hereford cattle on the Brighton Reservation, and 1,300 head of native cattle crossed with Brahman are raised on the Big Cypress Reservation. Stock-raising is fast becoming the main industry of the two reservations. (See Plate 7.)

On the Brighton Reservation many own their own saddle horses and milch cows, and on both of the reservations many families own hogs. Most of the hogs are the native razorback variety and are eaten by the Indians, though some are sold on the open market. Most of the Seminoles also keep chickens.

Very few of the Seminoles are farmers in the strict sense of the word. The Everglades is not a suitable place for farming. The Indians are not able to drain the swamps and apply the newer methods of agriculture. However, most have small gardens, where they raise corn, pumpkins, tomatoes, bananas, guavas, cowpeas, and sugar cane.

A sizable group of Seminoles find work in the labor market. Men and women help harvest truck-farm products such as beans, tomatoes, celery, and potatoes around the towns of Everglades and Okeechobee. Some have found employment in the gladiolus industry, and some work in the lumber camps and state road departments. Others find employment in commercial camps on the east coast, especially around Miami.

Some Seminoles make a living by staying in one of the fourteen villages along the Tamiami Trail between Fort Myers and Miami. These villages, hidden from view behind palisaded walls above which rise the sun-bleached palmetto-thatched roofs of native huts, or *chickees* (see Plate 8), are located opposite filling stations and are promoted by the filling-station owners, who transport the Indians to the sites along the highway and direct construction of the villages to attract sightseers. These Indians are free to come and go as they wish and are usually paid a small weekly wage.

In front of each village is a store or shop in which Seminole jackets, dolls, miniature boats, dresses, metal pins and buttons, shells, air plants, small tomtoms, postcards, and other native products are sold. (See Plates 8 and 9.) For a fee of about twenty-five cents visitors may enter the Seminole village to see the *chickees,* an alligator, a wildcat, and some raccoons. The men tend the store while the women sit in

Plate 17

A Seminole woman preparing the noonday meal.

Plate 18

A Seminole woman and a boy. Note her hat, the beads piled high around her neck, and the arrangement of her hair. Children usually do not wear hats.

Plate 19

Mary Osceola, with the usual beads, and with her hair arranged
in a manner typical among older Seminole women.

Plate 20

Charlie Billie, one of the few remaining Seminole medicine men,
in a traditional bright skirt that is now worn by few men.

Plate 21

Billy Bowlegs and Jessie Billie. Like most older men, Billy Bowlegs does not wear shoes.

Plate 22

Four Seminole girls.

Plate 23

Women preparing dinner over an open fire.

Plate 24

Seminole women preparing a kettleful of cane syrup.

Plate 25

A Seminole minister saying grace before the noonday meal is eaten.

Plate 26

The Independent Seminole Baptist Church on the Brighton Reservation.

Plate 27

Sunday-morning service at the Independent Baptist Church, with Charlie Bowers at the pulpit.

Plate 28

The Seminole Baptist Church just outside the Brighton Reservation.

Plate 29

The Glades Cross Indian Mission (Episcopal) at the town of Everglades.

Plate 30

Charlie Bowers and his wife and daughter; he is minister of the
Independent Baptist Church on Brighton Reservation.

Plate 31

Deaconess Harriet M. Bedell, Episcopal missionary at the Glades Cross Indian Mission at Everglades, Florida.

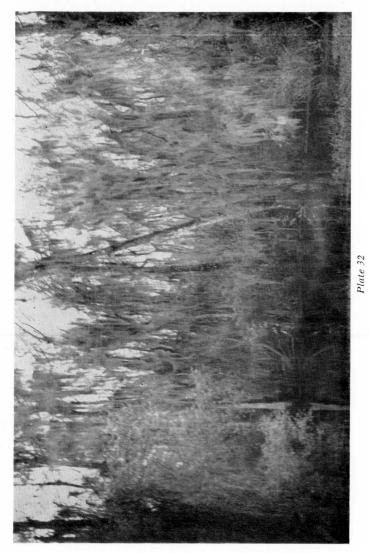

Plate 32

The cypress swamp.

their *chickees* and sew on hand-operated sewing machines (Plate 10).

Still other Seminoles make a living by hunting, fishing, trapping, acting as guides, and gathering frogs (see Plate 11). The economic status of the Seminoles has markedly improved in the past seventeen years, the per-capita wealth at the present time being nearly three times what it was in 1936.

All the Florida Seminoles live in shelters known as *chickees,* usually built with five to twelve cypress posts set in the ground, upon which a framework of light poles is constructed. On this framework is nailed a thatched roof of palmetto fronds that make a tight matting to keep out rain and sun. The sides of *chickees* are open except at night or during storms, when they are closed by placing canvas or cotton sheeting around the *chickees.* A platform raised about three feet from the ground forms a floor for sleeping and storing belongings. (See Plates 12 and 13.)

When the Seminole retires for the night, he places a few blankets on the raised platform of his *chickee,* then over him a blanket (in winter) or a sheet (in summer). This bedroll is pushed back during the day. A few Seminoles sleep on mattresses. The excellent health of the Seminoles may be attributed to their life in the open and the fact that their *chickees* are in reality open-air shelters.

A Seminole village consists of several *chickees* grouped together (Plate 14).

The truant officer is unknown among the Seminoles, for the State of Florida does not require Seminole children to attend school. Although segregation exists in Florida, as in other southern states, preventing Negro children from attend-

ing white schools and permitting white children to attend
only white schools, the law does not include the children of
the Seminoles. The Indian Agency located at Dania encour-
ages the Seminoles to send their children to white schools,
and teachers, parents of white children, and members of
local school boards have urged the Seminole children to come
to their schools. During the past five years the Seminoles
have shown much more interest in sending their children to
school than they have in the past.

There is a government school on the Brighton Indian
Reservation and another on the Big Cypress Reservation, in
each of which the first through the sixth grade are taught.
After the sixth grade is reached, children are urged to attend
public schools in near-by towns.

The teacher at the government school on the Brighton
Reservation is Mr. Bruce Boehmer, an excellent teacher and
of fine character, who has devoted his life to teaching and
helping the Indians. The nineteen pupils attending the
Brighton school are taught cattle-raising, and there is a small
herd of twenty-five school cattle. The pupils are also taught
manual training, learn how to make feedboxes, etc., and to
read, speak, and write English. (See Plates 15 and 16.)

The government school at the Big Cypress Reservation
has about twenty-five pupils, who are taught in the same way
as those at the Brighton Reservation.

Seminole children who wish to continue their education
attend the government school on the Cherokee Reservation in
North Carolina; twenty-five Seminole children are attending
the school at present. Those Seminoles who wish to become
ministers attend the Baptist Bible Institute at Lakeland,
Florida. Billy Osceola, the minister of the Brighton Indian
Baptist Church, which is located just outside the Brighton

Reservation, attended the Baptist Bible Institute for five years.

An old person among the Seminoles lives in the village of his closest woman relative, or he lives alone in a near-by friendly village. Old people keep track of their own personal property and care for their own vegetable gardens and live-stock. Old women do the work assigned them around the village, and old men bring in wood for the fire used for cooking. These old people stay in the villages while younger Seminoles are away, and care for the children, dogs, pigs, and chickens. Most Seminoles, because of environment, their lack of worry, their stoicism and belief in the inevitable, live to a ripe old age.

When a Seminole does wrong or breaks the tribal law he is punished by the tribal council. If he is convicted of lying, stealing or some other petty crime, he is steamed. A small tent is erected in the village; a hole is dug in the center of the tent and water placed in the hole. After heated stones are placed in the water, the culprit stands over the steaming waterhole. He is then confined to the village for four weeks. If he is convicted of murder, he is sentenced to death. That sentence has occurred only once in the past thirty years.

The act of June 2, 1924, (43 Stat. 253) provides that all Indians born within the territorial limits of the United States are citizens of the United States and of the state in which they reside, entitled to all the rights and privileges of citizenship, including the rights to vote, to hold public office, to buy, own, and dispose of personal and real property, and the right to execute valid contracts. But though all Indians are citizens of the United States, they are also wards of the Federal Government, and Federal laws forbid the barter, sale, or gift of intoxicating beverages to the Indians. Violations of this law are punishable by heavy penalties. In hunting and fishing, the Seminole Indians are subject to the laws of the State of Florida. Seminole boys must register when they reach draft age.

The population of the Florida Seminole Indians on February 2, 1953, as furnished by Kenneth A. Marmon (in charge of the Dania Indian Reservation), was 846. The population has increased; on January 1, 1940, the population was 590.

The problems of the Seminoles are covered with those of other citizens under the general benefits of the Social Security Act. All eligible Seminoles receive old-age assistance, and receive aid for dependent children. The State of Florida each year furnishes one hundred automobile license tags to the Seminoles without cost.

CHAPTER VII

The Seminole Way of Life

The language of the Seminole Indians, which originally had been Mikasuki, became predominantly Muskogee because of the influx of Indians of that tribe into Florida. The language was altered to such an extent that the Mikasuki Indians could not understand it. At the present time, the Seminoles on the Brighton Indian Reservation and west and north of Lake Okeechobee speak Muskogee. Those along the Tamiami Trail, on the Big Cypress Reservation, and on the Dania Reservation speak Mikasuki. The two languages are related, but someone speaking only one cannot understand the other.

All Seminoles speak in soft, low voices. When they talk among themselves their voices are so low at times that it sounds as if they are whispering rather than talking. The children talk quietly while they are at play, without any of the yelling and shrill cries heard among white children at play. Seminoles never yell at each other as white people do.

Children and younger Seminoles all speak quite good English, but older Indians as a rule do not understand or speak it. Some Seminoles can speak both Muskogee and Mikasuki. When they talk among themselves they always speak their own tongue. Only when they are visiting in the near-by towns, when the children attend school, or when some white visitor comes to their camp do they speak English.

The Seminoles do not make pottery or weave rugs or blankets as do other Indians living in North America. The men make silver ornaments for their own use, and the women make watch fobs out of beads. In every village are mechanical sewing machines with which the women make dolls, moccasins, and dresses. These Indian dolls, made of native material and cloth, represent Seminole women and men. Sport shirts, aprons, and Seminole women's costumes are made to order, and a small amount of woodcarving and basketwork is done.

Seminole clothing, with its bright-colored designs, may have been adopted centuries ago. The Peruvian Indians of South America wore costumes similar to those of the Seminoles hundreds of years ago, and a tradition says that the patterns used on Seminole women's dresses are similar to those found on sea shells on the beaches along the Atlantic and Gulf of Mexico.

Women's garments are composed of hundreds of patches of cloth pieced into stripes that, when sewed together, form horizontal varicolored bands which reach from the waist to the ground. The skirt may consist of as many as five thousand separate pieces of cloth. Every Seminole woman wears a long skirt which wraps around her feet, a clever device to protect her as she trudges through the scrub and palmetto. Women turn their feet in slightly as they kick their skirts in front of them to avoid stepping on them. The movement gives them a peculiar waddling walk. Since they do not wear any undergarments, by lifting their skirts they can wade through water without wetting their clothing.

The women also wear capes and, at times, blouses under the capes. The cape is usually made of cloth of a solid color, in contrast to the many-colored skirt, and extends to just below the waist, forming the upper part of the dress.

This dress, which is sewed and made on a hand-operated sewing machine (Plate 10), assures the women perfect comfort. The full, loose costume keeps off the sun and is perfect for the hot, humid climate, for it does not stick to the skin.

The younger women wear their hair long and loose (see Plates 17 and 23); however, some Indian women living in both the Brighton and the Big Cypress reservations have within the last five or six years adopted a new way of wearing their hair inspired by the brim of a hat. This is another example of the way in which they have adapted themselves to their environment, for their hair acts as an eye-shade. A piece of cardboard cut somewhat in the shape of a hat brim is covered and the edge wired. After the hair is drawn to the top of the head and tied there like a switch, the brim is fastened on securely. The hair is always in perfect order, and the "hat" is a great comfort in the dry season and on sunny days. This type of hat is usually worn when Seminole women visit near-by towns and cities. (See Plate 18.)

A few of the older women gather their hair to one side and hold it in place by a net, and some older Seminole women have bangs in front and a knot in the back (see Plate 19).

Many women still wear pounds and pounds of beads around their necks, but Seminole girls usually wear only a few strings of beads (Plate 22).

Only a very few Seminole men at the present time still wear a two-piece costume consisting of a blouse and skirt (see Plate 20). Most of them wear pants with either a bright-colored shirt made by the Seminole women or a white man's shirt (see Plate 21). Many wear tennis shoes or sneakers instead of moccasins or shoes. Some of the older men go barefooted, and children and younger boys and girls all go barefooted. A few old Seminole men still wear turbans, but most of them either go bareheaded or wear ten-gallon cowboy hats. A very few have their heads shaved, but most have the same haircuts as the white men.

Seminole girls dress much like their mothers, in long, bright-colored skirts, and with a few strands of beads around their necks (see Plate 22).

Young Seminole boys wear the old-fashioned skirts but are given overalls as they grow older.

The Seminoles eat well. But they are subject to the hunting and fishing laws of the State of Florida, and as the Everglades have been developed, notably around the towns of Everglades and Okeechobee, the hunting and fishing is not what it used to be.

The Indians cook over an open fire. In the center of a Seminole village is the fireplace built of eight or ten dry logs arranged like the spokes of a wheel. The fire is built at the hub, and as the ends are consumed the logs are pushed nearer the blaze. The unburned ends of the logs provide convenient seats near the fire. In one large Indian village on the Brighton Reservation an iron grate 4 by 7 feet supported by four tin cans is used for preparing the food (see Plate 23).

At times the Seminoles erect over the open cooking fire a roof thatched with palmetto leaves or fronds supported by four uprights set in the ground. Besides protecting the fire, this structure serves as a kitchen house and shelter in bad weather. The rafters form convenient places on which family pots and pans are hung when not in use, and the smoke from the fire tends to preserve dry meats and herbs hung from the rafters. Near by is another *chickee* containing a large table with pails and pans for preparing the food.

A large iron kettle is used for cooking most of the food that the Seminoles eat. Wild turkeys, rabbits, curlews, herons, gophers, venison, beef, pork, and, rarely, veal or mutton find their way into this kettle and are eaten as stews. The staple food of the Seminoles is *sofkee,* a mush made of ground corn meal. They prepare flour from the coonite and chinbrier obtained from the jungle, and corn, sweet potatoes, Irish potatoes, pumpkins, mellons, squash, and cowpeas are raised near the permanent villages. The bud of the cabbage palm is either eaten raw or cooked; cocoa plums, sour oranges, sea grapes, guavas, bananas, gopher apples, and mangroves grow wild and are gathered in season.

For sweetening used in their food, the Seminoles depend a great deal on syrup obtained from small patches of sugar cane planted near their settlements or villages (see Plate 24). However, some purchase sugar, as well as canned food, from the near-by towns.

After the food is prepared, it is placed on individual plates, which are then placed on a large wooden table around which the Indians gather. The food is blessed (Plate 25), and they then take their food and eat it in their *chickees,* some sitting crosslegged, others eating on raised platforms out in the open.

Seminoles drink very little tea, but coffee is served with many of their meals. They consume large amounts of soft drinks and obtain their drinking water from holes dug in the swamp, from driven wells in the permanent villages, or from near-by towns, from which the water is transported in large milk cans or metal drums (see Plate 12).

Though there are a few garbage pails in each Indian village, dogs, chickens, and pigs dispose of most waste material.

The present diet of the Seminoles is definitely overloaded with meat and starch. They eat few fresh vegetables, they do not drink milk or eat butter. Much of their dental trouble arises from the nature of the food that they eat.

Seminole children are just as fond of games as white children are. They play checkers, marbles, hide-and-seek, and ball. Little Seminole girls skip rope and make mud pies. At an early age the children are given a share of the family property; they have their own chickens, pigs, and vegetable gardens, and what they make from these enterprises belongs to them. At the Brighton School is a playground where the boys and girls swing beneath the oak trees and play ball.

The majority of Seminole songs are sung at the Green-Corn Dance (see Chapter IX). The Snake Song, the Horned Owl Song, and the Hunting Dance Song are frequently sung; and songs are sung at the Alligator, Catfish, Quail, and Screech Owl dances. Seminole women often sing as they work and sing or chant lullabies to their babies. Medicine men sing and chant when they treat the sick. And Seminole children often sing while playing.

There are very few musical instruments used in connection with their songs, though the Seminoles sing church hymns without accompaniment. Rattles made from cocoanut shells, turtle shells, and tin cans are used during singing, and tomtoms are also used during the singing and dancing. Occasionally a cane flute is played, but very rarely.

CHAPTER VIII

Christianity Among the Seminoles

As in education, the Seminoles remain in religion a reticent people, hesitating to adopt the ways of the white man. A Seminole will sit and listen to a white man's opinions and afterwards do as he pleases. Older Indians still cling to their old rites and customs, and most of the Seminoles still believe in the Great Spirit. Ghosts are very real to them. Billy Bowlegs, living near the town of Everglades, told of seeing two ghosts while driving along a country road one night; when he stopped his car the ghosts vanished. Seminoles prefer any form of death to hanging, for they believe that the spirit leaves the body by the mouth and that when a person is hanged the spirit remains imprisoned in the body. The younger Seminoles attend churches on the Indian reservations, but very few have adopted the Christian religion.

The first Seminole Baptist Church was built with contributed materials by Indians at the Dania Reservation and dedicated in the summer of 1936. In charge of the ceremonies was Holy Canard, an Indian from Oklahoma, who distributed printed business cards declaring that he held a formal commission from the President of the United States as principal chief of the Creek nation.

The Independent Baptist Church of twenty-five members, all from one village, is located on the Brighton Reservation. The church is built like their native *chickees,* a roof made of palmetto fronds supported by cypress posts and with a dirt floor. The pews are packing boxes and collapsible chairs, and the pulpit is a cypress pole with a board nailed on the bottom for support and another on the top to hold the Bible. From the rafters hang two pictures of Christ. (See Plates 26 and 27.)

The minister, Nick (Charlie) Bowers (see Plate 30), a Seminole, has not attended any religious school or seminary but is one of the most intelligent Indians in the village and acts as their leader as well as their minister. Every Sunday morning they hold Sunday school and morning service in their church, which is located about half a mile from the paved highway that runs through the reservation. The congregation sings hymns in the native tongue without the assistance of an organ or piano. The minister, who also speaks very good English, preaches and prays in the Muskogee language. From time to time members of the congregation rise and read from a prayerbook, sometimes speaking in English and sometimes in Muskogee. During the Sunday-morning service, which lasts about an hour, dogs, chickens, and pigs wander into the church and are chased out by the Indians. Children, especially the smaller ones, go and come as they please; when these children become too noisy they are admonished by the older women.

These Seminoles take their religion very seriously. I have never attended a white church where the members showed more devotion, sincerity, and faith than the Indians showed when I attended their service one Sunday morning. They prefer their own church and their own minister and do not attend or support the Brighton Indian Baptist Church located only about a mile away off the reservation.

The Brighton Indian Baptist Church, just off the Brighton Reservation, a small one-room building which will seat 150 people, is made of cinder blocks painted white (see Plate 28). There are six windows on either side and a front and back door, and at the front is a platform with pulpit, chair, and bench seating seven people. The church is comfortably furnished with benches on either side. At the back there is a large gray desk on which pamphlets printed in English are placed for the congregation to take and read. Just in front of the pulpit is a little gray table that holds the song books and two Indian-made collection plates. The church has electric lights and a large electric fan, which keeps the church comfortable at all times.

The pastor of the Brighton Indian Baptist Church, Billy Osceola, a Seminole ordained minister, who has had five years of study at the Baptist Bible Institute at Lakeland, Florida, is married and has two children. The Rev. Billy Osceola is assisted in his work by the Rev. Willie King, a retired Creek Indian missionary, and by the Rev. Fred Brooks, a Baptist missionary who with his wife came from the Highland Park Baptist Church in Chattanooga, Tennessee, a few years ago to do missionary work among the Indians on the Brighton Reservation.

The religious activities at this church each Lord's Day begin with Sunday school, attended by thirty Seminoles ranging from babies in arms to adults. Some of the classes are taught by the Seminoles. Following Sunday school is a church service, with forty Indians attending. At six o'clock there is a training union for young Seminoles, and every Monday evening there is choir practice. Seminoles like to sing, and attendence is always good at these choir rehearsals. On each third Sunday there is an all-day meeting at the church, with dinner and supper cooked and served on the church grounds.

The Rev. Fred Brooks and his wife, who live in the town of Okeechobee, some twenty-five miles from the Brighton Indian Reservation, have done a wonderful work among the Seminoles on the reservation. They are inspired by God and are teaching the Indians to love, fear, and respect the Almighty as no other missionaries in recent times. As time goes on, their good work will continue, and they will be rewarded by the progress of these Indians in Christian ways of life.

Indians living on the Brighton Reservation, called Muskogee Indians or Creek Indians, attend either the Independent Baptist Church or the Brighton Indian Baptist Church. The Mikasuki Indians, living in commercial villages along the Tamiami Trail, in villages along the Immokalee Road, and in their own villages in the Big Cypress Reservation, are taught Christianity by the Episcopal Church. In 1898 the Glades Cross Episcopal Mission was established at Boat Landing in the Everglades by Bishop Gray. There were several baptisms, but these have all died and Boat Landing is no more. Older Indians still remember Dr. Golden, who bought a store at Boat Landing and conducted the Mission Hotel after Bishop Gray died.

Some years after Dr. Golden died the Glades Cross Episcopal Mission was built at Everglades, Florida. This mission, a one-story frame building containing six rooms (Plate 29), provides living quarters for Deaconess Harriet M. Bedell

(Plate 31), the Episcopal missionary, and space for storing the dresses, dolls, and beadwork brought to the mission by Seminole women. There are sold by Deaconess Bedell, and the Seminole women receive slips of paper entitling them to purchase food at the stores in the town of Everglades. The property on which the mission stands was given the diocese by the Collier Corporation. The work at the Glades Cross Episcopal Mission covers a wide territory extending along the Tamiami Trail eighty miles to Miami, seventy-two miles west to Fort Myers, and forty miles north to Immokalee, and to villages out in the Everglades and south on Turner River.

Deaconess Harriet M. Bedell in charge of this vast area is a most remarkable woman. At the age of seventy-seven, though retired, she still carries on. She began her missionary work among the Eskimos in Alaska and has worked at the Glades Cross Episcopal Mission for the past thirty years. She is a devout Christian woman who has spent her life trying to help others and to spread the word of God; surely her reward will be great when she enters the Kingdom of Heaven. Her work consists of visits to the Indian villages and industrial work that helps the Indians to be self-supporting, develops their native arts and crafts, and makes contacts for knowing them better and winning them for Christ and His Church.

Through the kindness of friends and the Collier Corporation, there is an Indian village where the Indians gather from time to time for group work, house parties, Christmas, and other festivals. One Indian family lives in the village and acts as caretakers. There are a large assembly building built by the Indians and several family *chickees*.

Scarcely a day passes that Indians do not come to the mission bringing their needlework dresses and dolls to exchange for slips of paper for the purchase of food, to tell

Deaconess Bedell about some sickness in the family or the arrival of a new baby. When a new baby is born, blankets are given and a prayer is offered. Should the baby die, Deaconess Bedell offers a prayer at the funeral and accompanies the family to a grave near the Indian village or to a grave in the Indian cemetery in the town of Everglades.

CHAPTER IX

Seminole Legends, Customs and Beliefs

During the hour before falling asleep, and while the embers of the campfire are softly glowing, parents tell the legends and stories of the past to their listening family. The wild animals of the Everglades, the forces of nature, and heavenly bodies are usually endowed with speech in these stories, which for charm, sentiment, and beauty of expression compare favorably with the folklore of other races.

One story often told by the elders to their children tells how, when the white, black, and red men had been created, they were very poor, with no traps, weapons, or tools with which to kill game. One day while the three were looking up into the sky, three boxes floated down to earth to greet them and the voice of the Great Spirit was heard. The Great Spirit commanded the white man to look into the boxes and choose one of them for his portion. The white man opened the boxes and selected one containing pens, a compass, and such things as people use now. The red man, given the second choice, chose the box containing tomahawks, knives, clubs, and traps—all things used in war and hunting. The box filled with axes, hoes, buckets for carrying water, and whips for driving oxen was allotted by the Great Spirit to the Negro. This meant that his people must work for the white people and the Indians.

Another story concerns three men who stopped beside a small pool to bathe. The first man came out clean, and his descendants are all white people. Because the water had been dirtied, the second man emerged from the pool not quite so clean; and his descendants are Indians. The water was very dirty by this time, and when the third man came from the pool he was black; his people are Negroes.

There is still another legend among the Seminoles that the Great Spirit fashioned men out of clay. He overbaked the first batch, who came out black and burned, the Negroes. The next batch were underbaked and came out pale—the white man. In the next attempt the Great Spirit created fresh models, subjected them to just the right amount of baking, and they came out a perfect color—the Indians.

Although one may become very friendly with the Seminoles, there is always a point beyond which the white man cannot pass. Many of the rites, customs, and beliefs are not discussed outside the tribe. All that goes on during the tribal council is never divulged, nor is the training of the medicine man.

However, we do know the duties of the medicine man and his place formerly in the life and culture of the Seminoles. The priests, or medicine men, were important chiefly as virtuous Indians; they had to be good in the Indian sense if they were to inherit the powerful bundles of the highest rank, the *yaholi*. These bundles I have never been permitted to see, although I have talked to Indians who possess them. The medicine men had to go through years of preparation of prayer and fasting with their elders until they became plain doctors, or "medicine grandfathers." In some cases, for practical work with childbearing, Seminole women were also doctors, as well as the medicine men.

The medicine men were supposed to be able to heal with brews of herbs, sweet bay, willow, cedar leaf, snakeroot, and other herbs, by chanting or sucking the evil from the patient's forehead. Cured in this manner were such diseases as rat sickness, mosquito sickness, and fever caused by dreams of fire or of the bear, or distracted wandering called "the giant disease." The magic of the medicine men had to be strong and to protect warriors in battle and bring weakness to their enemies. The Indians had to be strong in peace, obeying the rituals. If they failed, new magic had to be obtained.

At a certain time in a Seminole boy's life he is taken to the camp of the medicine man and given an emetic similar to the ancient black drink. He is then taken out into the jungle with the medicine man and stays there for ten days, during which time he studies God and nature. During this period he does not eat solid food but subsists on a brew made of herbs. He then returns to the camp of the medicine man, where he receives solid food. This training goes on from four to ten years, depending on the ability of the Seminole boy to learn and absorb the teachings of the medicine man. (This is an old custom; few Seminole boys today practice this form of learning. Instead, they attend schools at the Brighton Indian Reservation and the Big Cypress Indian Reservation.)

There are very few medicine men among the Seminoles today. The only one known to any extent is Charlie Billie, who lives in an Indian village near Miami (see Plate 20).

There is a legend concerning crystal springs, of which there are many in Florida. Eternal youth was not to be found in the crystal depths of Florida's springs, but their mysterious caverns provide a source of much lore among the Seminoles. On moonlight nights hundreds of little people only four inches high came and danced in these caverns, until a huge Indian warrior in a stone canoe appeared and drove them away. This illusion was created perhaps by waving water plants and the moving shadow from a projecting rock in the springs.

Another legend concerns the saw grass of the Everglades. When pollen of the saw grass is seen floating in the air, the Seminoles seek higher ground, knowing that a hurricane is coming. During the 1926 and 1928 storms no Indians were reported drowned. It is not the providental blooming of the saw grass that foretells a storm but an atmospheric condition that makes the pollen visible for several days before the hurricane arrives.

The most important ritual in the life of the Seminoles is the meeting of the tribal council and the Green-Corn Dance that occurs each year in July or August. The Seminoles living on the Brighton Indian Reservation and around the northern end of Lake Okeechobee and those on the Big Cypress Indian Reservation hold separate meetings of the tribal council and separate Green-Corn Dances. Those on the Brighton Indian Reservation send delegates to the tribal council of the Big Cypress Reservation, but the Cypress Indians do not send delegates to the council of the Brighton Indians.

The tribal council and its Green-Corn Dance is a truly democratic body in which not only the men but all the women over eighteen have a voice. All judicial matters, such as decreeing punishment, even the death sentence, are handled in the council, and all marriages and divorces are passed on during the meeting.

Billy Smith is one of the most prominent Seminoles in the tribal council of the Brighton Indians, while Billy Motola, Cuffney Tiger, Ingram Billy, and Josse Billy are prominent in the tribal council at Big Cypress.

The precise date of the Green-Corn Dance is fixed by the chief and his associates and is determined by how early or late corn ripens. The Green-Corn Dance usually lasts eight days, though at times only four days. Early in the morning of the first day the men clean the yard and sprinkle white sand around. Then they bring in four large logs that are placed in the center of the square to form a cross, the outer ends pointing to the cardinal points of the compass. In the center of the cross a fire is made that will burn for about four days.

During the first day the Turkey Dance is performed by women of the turkey tribe. While the women are dancing, the *possau,* a powerful emetic to be drunk by all the Indians during the afternoon, is brewed. Following the Turkey Dance, four men and four women dance the Tadpole Dance. In the evening the men dance *E-ne-hou-bun-gau* until eleven o'clock at night.

During the second day the women dance the *Its-ho-bun-gau-gun* Dance. At noon the men take ashes from the fire and rub them on their chins, necks, and bellies and jump into the river. When they then return to the village, the women having prepared corn for the feast, the men take some of the corn and rub it between their hands, on their faces, breasts, and necks. Then all the Seminoles feast.

The third day, they just sit around recovering from the feast of the day before. On the fourth day the women go early in the morning to get logs for a new fire. Then they sprinkle white sand around the yard. The men take ashes from the old fire, rub them on their chins, necks, and bellies, and jump into the river. All eat salt this day and dance the long dance.

On the fifth day they build a new fire and drink a concoction, *cassine yupon,* and on the sixth and seventh days they just sit around.

On the eighth day the Indians get three large pots and some physic plants, which are placed in the pots with water and heated until the water boils. Old corncobs and pine burs are collected and placed in a pot and burned to ashes. Four virgins who have not begun having menses bring ashes from their *chickees,* put them in the pots, and mix them with the ashes of corncobs and pine burs. The men take white clay and mix it with water in pans. One pan of clay and some of the ashes are taken to the *chickee* of the chief, and the other pan and the rest of the ashes are distributed among the men. They then rub themselves with clay and ashes. Some tobacco flowers are brought in, and the chief and the tribal council go four times around the fire, every time as they face east throwing some of the tobacco flowers into the fire. They then stand facing west. The men then repeat the same ceremony.

During the festival large quantities of food are consumed and many logs are burned. Like many other customs among the Seminoles, the Green-Corn Dance is in process of decay. Once attendance at this festival was mandatory, but now fewer and fewer attend. Although there is much drinking, dancing, purging, and feasting at this festival, nothing objectionable has ever been reported.

Every four years a hunting dance is held in the fall by Brighton and Big Cypress Indians.

When two Seminoles decide to get married, the women-folk of the groom's family provide the bedding for the couple, and some woman relative of the bride sews the groom a bright-colored shirt. Marriages are confirmed by the tribal council at the Green-Corn Dance. After the ceremony (which never takes place in a white man's church or civil court) the groom takes up his residence with the bride and her family. The groom may stay with his wife's people for years and, as his family grows, may find himself a hammock near by and there build a new *chickee* for himself and his family.

There is some intermarriage between the Indians living on the Big Cypress Reservation and those living on the Brighton Reservation, but there are few intermarriages between the two groups of Indians. The Seminoles do not forbid intermarriage with the whites, but only five Seminoles at the present time have either white wives or white husbands.

Practically all marriages endure. In 1916 there was only one divorced couple among the Seminoles. As in the marriage, the tribal council at the Green-Corn Dance makes the final decision regarding the merits or demerits of the divorce. When a divorce is decided upon the husband gets out and the wife and children remain with her relatives. Federal law recognizes these marriages and divorces.

Though the Seminoles have been forced for many years to choose their mates from a distinctly limited group, thus really inbreeding among themselves, there is at the present time no evidence of deterioration of the race.

Seminole women and children are buried in the swamps near their villages, but all the adult males are buried in the remote jungle. A male is placed in a crude casket and then is carried to some hidden place in the jungle, where the casket is set down, above ground, is surrounded by logs cut from the cabbage palm to make a sort of fence around the body, and fronds of cabbage palm placed over the casket.

The bodies of the chiefs at times are placed in hollow logs or trees, or on low platforms, the bodies protected from birds and animals by a cover of logs cut from cabbage palms. Personal possessions of the Seminoles are often placed near the body.

When a famous Seminole dies, the campfire is kept going to ward off evil spirits. All his possessions are moved and placed near his body, and the women of the village let down their hair as a sign of grief and the family of the deceased moves to a new *chickee*. After about five days, during which the campfire smolders and the widow remains secluded with her children and eats little, the campfire no longer burns, and the evil spirits have departed. The widow comes out of seclusion and removes all the beads from around her neck. She must remain a widow for five moons. Seminoles pray that the spirits of the departed will remain in the spirit land and not return to wander among the living, and thus bring misfortune.

Within the past few years many Seminoles have requested that their dead be buried in the government cemetery on the Dania Reservation. These burials are conducted by the missionaries. In addition to the cemetery at the Dania Reservation, there is a cemetery at Everglades, Florida, provided for the Indians by the Glades Cross Episcopal Mission. In time, no doubt, cemeteries for the Indians will be established on both the Brighton and the Big Cypress Indian reservations.

CHAPTER X

The Future of the Seminoles

The Seminole population is increasing. They are becoming more educated, and most of them speak English. The Seminoles are seeking the service of the medicine man less and less and are depending more and more on two physicians, one living in the town of Okeechobee and the other in Miami, both under contract by the Government to care for the Indians in those two areas. The Seminoles attend and enjoy movies and more and more are mixing with the white people living in the Everglades.

These white people, those living in Fort Myers, Naples, Okeechobee, Everglades, Immokalee, and Miami have a very definite obligation regarding the Seminoles. In Immokalee there is not even a moving-picture theater; when Seminoles go to Immokalee, there is nothing for them to do but get drunk. Each town and city should have recreation centers set aside for the Seminoles, as the larger towns have chambers of commerce with shuffle boards and other diversions where tourists from the North gather and enjoy themselves. In these recreation centers there should be a hostess and games provided for the Seminoles. If recreation centers were established, the Seminoles would go there instead of to some tavern to purchase liquor.

This mingling of the Seminoles with the white man will increase as time goes on, and the white man must meet the challenge. If met in the proper manner, with recreation centers and places of amusement in the larger cities and towns, the Seminoles will contribute positively to the culture and growth of southern Florida. If nothing is done by these communities and the Seminoles are permitted to loiter, drink, and carouse in these cities and towns, their race will deteriorate. They will acquire more of the white man's diseases, the white man's taste for liquor, and the white man's morals. They will then become, instead, a definite burden to the people living in southern Florida.

Bibliography

Douglas, Marjory Stoneman, *The Everglades, River of Grass.* New York: Reinhart.

Fletcher, Sydney, *A Survey of the Seminole Indians of Florida.*

Florida: A Guide to the Southernmost State, compiled and written by the Federal Writers' Project of the Works Progress Administration for the State of Florida.

Hanna, Katheryn A., *Florida, Land of Change.* Chapel Hill: University of North Carolina Press.

McKenny, Thomas L., and James Hall, *History of the Indian Tribes of North America.*

Neail, Wilfred T., *Florida Seminole Indians.* Ocala, Fla.: Taylor Printing Co.

"1953: Everglades National Park in Florida," published by the Department of the Interior.

"1953: Florida Board of Parks and Historical Memorials," published by the State of Florida.

Verill, A. Hyatt, *Romantic and Historical Florida.*

DATE DUE

F			
NOV 22 '66			
DEC 10 '69			
GAYLORD			PRINTED IN U.S.A.